Contents

Page no.

Published by Bletchley Park Trust 2008.

Breaking German Naval Enigma

(Some of the additional difficulties and how they were resolved.)

Introduction

It has been said that at the beginning of the war the only persons in Bletchley Park who believed the Naval Enigma could be broken were Frank Birch, later to become the head of the Naval Section, and the mathematician Alan Turing. The general lack of optimism at this time could seem to have been justified by the fact that for the first 18 months of the war no German Naval ciphers were broken.

The fact that by the third week of January 1940 BP had experienced its first success in breaking the Enigma ciphers of the German Air Force shows clearly that there were additional formidable problems that had to be solved before the Naval ciphers could be broken.

The two objectives of this short report are to explain briefly what these difficulties were and to provide some details of the methods that were used to resolve them. The historical details of related events that occurred at sea will not be addressed here.

It is assumed that the reader is already familiar with the structure and properties of a 3-rotor Enigma machine, and of the role of the Bombes in breaking Enigma ciphers by means of cribs.

It will helpful to begin by comparing the enciphering procedure used by the German Air Force and Army with that used by the German Navy.

The Procedure used by the German Army and Air Force:-

The Army and Air Force operators were equipped with a 3-rotor Enigma machine together with a set of five different rotors. Each day, according to the instructions given in the current monthly '*setting sheet*', the operators would install the three specified rotors in their machines in the prescribed order, so that any one of 60 possible '*rotor orders*' could have been used. The '*setting sheet*' also specified the ring-settings for the day and the ten pairs of letters (known as the '*steckers*') that the operators were to connect up on the plug-board at the front of the machine.

The set of daily instructions given in the '*setting sheet*' were referred to as the '*key for the day*', and the Enigma configuration used to encipher a particular message consisted of the '*key for the day*' together with the initial rotor starting positions or *'message settings'* that had been used. The latter were chosen independently by the sending operator so that each message had its own individual *'message settings'*.

It was of course essential for the operator receiving the signal to know the *'message settings'*, and this information had to be included in the transmitted signal, but in a way that concealed it from the British. This was achieved by including in a preface to the cipher-text, two groups of three letters, known at BP as the *'indicator setting'* and the *'indicator'* formulated by the operator in the following way. Having configured his Enigma machine to the prescribed *'key for the day'*, the operator chose an arbitrary group of three letters (say GSN) to use as the *'indicator setting'*, and turned the three rotors in his machine (left, middle, right) to these positions. He then chose a second arbitrary group of three letters (say QNK) as the required *'message setting'* and enciphered these three letters on his Enigma machine, the three cipher letters illuminated in turn on the lamp panel (say HAZ), forming the *'indicator'* for the message.

The operator receiving the signal recovered the unknown *'message settings'* by first turning the three rotors in his machine to the received *'indicator setting'* (GSN) and then enciphering the three letters of the received *'indicator'* (HAZ) on his machine, thus recovering the *message setting* QNK. (The outcome QNK is the result of the reciprocal properties of the Enigma machine.)

Breaking the Army and Air Force Enigma messages:

From the end of August 1940, after the Bombe had become operational, the standard technique for breaking these cipher messages depended upon finding an accurate crib for one selected message. From this crib a corresponding menu was set up on the bombe and trial runs were then made with different rotor orders to find the Bombe 'stops' one of which would ultimately provide the Enigma *'key for the day'*, and also the *'message settings'* for the message that had been selected.

In a worst case scenario this would require sixty bombe runs to be made to cover all the possible rotor orders. The Bombe run time for a single rotor order was about 18 minutes, so the total time required to find the key would under these worst circumstances have been about 18 x 60 minutes (18 hours).

However once the *'key for the day'* had been recovered from the one message that had been selected, **all** the other messages sent on the same key could then be easily deciphered because the *'message settings'* could be recovered directly from their indicators using the '*key for the day*', in exactly the same way as the German operators were doing.

The use of the Bombe depended entirely upon cribs and for these to be forthcoming it was necessary to have experience of the nature of the plain-text from previously broken messages. In the case of the Air Force this was not a major problem as from the end of May 1940, as a consequence of lapses in security by some of the German Enigma operators, BP had managed to break their ciphers almost every day. In the case of the German Army ciphers it was much more difficult as the Army imposed a higher level of security when formulating their messages and the proportion of signals that were broken was not as high.

The Procedure used by the German Navy

At the beginning of the war the German Navy were using the 3-rotor M3 Enigma machine that was similar to the version used by other two branches of the Armed services. However in addition to the five standard rotors used by the other two services, the Navy operators were equipped with three special 'Naval rotors'. This meant the total number of possible rotor orders available for use was increased from 60 to 336.

Like their colleagues in the other two services, the Navy operators were issued with monthly '*setting sheets*' that gave instructions on how the keys were to be set up on their Enigma machines, but the details were somewhat different. The Naval sheets specified the rotor order and the ring-settings that were to be used for pairs of days for the month covered by the sheet, (this part of the key was known as the '*inner settings*').

The '*outer settings*', which were changed every day, consisted of the ten specified '*stecker*' letter pairs together with a prescribed set of special positions for the three rotors known as the '*Grundstellung*'.

The '*message setting*' for each message, were not independently chosen by the operator, instead he was required to select a group of three letters known as the '*procedure indicator group*' from a designated section of a printed book (the '*K-Book*'). He then obtained the three letters of the '*message settings*' by turning the three rotors in his Enigma machine to the prescribed '*Grundstellung*' positions, and then enciphering on it the three letters of the '*procedure indicator group*'. The three letters illuminated in turn on the lamp panel giving the '*message settings*'. (At BP any messages that had been enciphered in this way were referred to collectively as '**Dolphin**'.)

Just like the other two Services an indicator system was used to enable the recipient operator to recover the *'message settings'*, but the following more complex procedure was used:-

The *'procedure indicator group'* obtained from the K-book was enciphered, not on the Enigma machine, but by means of an independent hand method using a set of *'bi-gram'* tables provided for the purpose. The hand-enciphered indicator obtained in this way was included twice in the transmitted signal, once in front of the cipher-text and again after it.

The recipient, also having a set of these bi-gram tables, used them to recover the original *'procedure indicator group'* and from this he could derive the *'message settings'* by using his Enigma machine just as the sending operator had done.

An illustrative example of this rather lengthy procedure is given in appendix (i), and some information about the bi-gram tables that were used is given in appendix (ii).

The problems encountered in breaking 'Dolphin'.

From the beginning of the war until about May 1941 very little was known about how the plain-text of the Naval messages had been formulated and consequently there were no reliable cribs available to use with the Bombe.

Even supposing that accurate cribs had been available, the problem of dealing with the very big increase in the number of possible rotor orders (from 60 to 336) would have caused serious logistical difficulties. When 336 rotor orders have to be taken into account the corresponding Bombe run time is approximately 336 x 18 minutes (i.e. in excess of 4 days), and this length of time would have seriously compromised the value of any of the intelligence derived from the signals. In theory the time could have been reduced by dividing up the work between several Bombes, however at the end of 1940 BP only had two of these machines available for all of the daily tasks it was attempting to deal with.

Furthermore even if the Enigma key for a given day had been found from the successful breaking of one of the intercepted messages, the Naval indicator procedure in use prevented the direct recovery of the *'message settings'* from the indicators of the other signals sent on that day, as was done for the signals of the Army and Air Force.

Resolving these problems:

At the time it was very evident to those involved that there was no way out of this difficult situation until of one of the German monthly setting sheets had been captured. It was also realised that it would be necessary to increase greatly the number of operational Bombes in order to effectively exploit such a capture.

The first capture of a setting sheet occurred in the spring of 1941 and this enabled some progress to be made, as the '*key for the day*' was now known for a limited number of days. However there remained the problem of finding the individual message settings of the intercepted signals, as these could not be directly determined until the bi-gram tables had been captured or painstakingly recovered by means of cryptography. This problem was initially resolved by constructing each day what became known as an '*EINS catalogue*'.

At the time it was believed that the four letter group 'EINS' was the one likely to occur most often in the plain-text of German Naval messages. This assumption was in fact correct as later it was confirmed that about 90% of the plain-text messages did contain at least one 'EINS' group of letters.

The daily catalogue consisted of a list of the four letter groups obtained by enciphering the letter group EINS at all 17,576 positions of the rotors, using the key of the day provided by the captured setting sheets.

The cipher text of the messages intercepted on that day could then be compared with the entries in the corresponding catalogue to see if any of the four letter groups listed in it also occurred in the cipher-texts. If such a repeat was found then it indicated that with a particular set of rotor positions, the four characters of the cipher message would decipher to the plain-text 'EINS'. Whenever this occurred then further letters from the cipher sequence were 'deciphered' to see if more letters of German plain-text was obtained. In fact it was found that about one quarter of these checks did provide the necessary confirmation, and for these cases the original message settings could then be readily determined.

The daily construction of the catalogues was a prodigious task, initially carried out by hand! Later a machine known as 'the Baby' was used, this recorded all of the entries on to punched cards, so that the lengthy process of comparing the entries in the catalogue with the cipher messages could be 'automated' thus greatly reducing the time taken.

A small part of an EINS catalogue is given in Appendix (iii) together with a simple example to demonstrate how it was used.

Recovering the Bi-gram tables

This somewhat convoluted procedure is not well documented. However it appears that on days when the number of *message settings* found by means of the EINS catalogue was sufficiently large (about 200 or so) then it was probable that a few of the hand enciphered indicators of the messages would be found to contain common pairs of letters, and these could be used as a basis for a systematic search to determine the *'Grundstellung'* settings for that day.

Once the *'Grundstellung'* for a particular day had been recovered, then the *'procedure indicators'* for the messages intercepted on that day could be recovered directly from the corresponding *'message settings'* that had been obtained by means of the EINS catalogue.

The recovery of the Bi-gram tables was then possible by carrying out (over a period of time) a laborious process that involved making comparisons between the recovered *'procedure indicators'* and the corresponding letter groups given in the intercepted signals.

Some of the broken messages were a source of reliable cribs for other subsequently intercepted messages that could be tested on the Bombes. However, bearing in mind the limited resources available, there remained the serious logistical difficulty caused by the large number of rotor orders that had to be tested.

Banburismus:

To overcome this difficulty, Alan Turing devised a highly ingenious technique known as *'Banburismus'* , that could greatly reduce the number of rotor orders that had to be checked on the Bombes, however before it could be applied it was essential that first the Bi-gram tables currently being used had been recovered.

'Banburismus' was laborious and labour intensive technique but its use made it possible to identify the rotors that had NOT been used in certain positions in the Enigma machine on a particular pair of days, and this lead to a spectacular reduction to the number of rotor orders that had to be tested on the Bombes.

The use of this technique ceased in September 1943 as by this date the number of Bombes available had increased considerably and it had become feasible to test the cribs without imposing any restrictions on the number of wheel orders that could to be tested.

A more detailed description of 'Banburismus' is given in Appendix (iv).

Naval Cribs:

There were three types of crib used to find the Naval Enigma keys.

(i) 'Straight' cribs, (ii) 'Depth' cribs, (iii) Cribs derived from 're-encodements'.

'Straight' cribs:- As the name might suggest, this type of crib was a conjecture (i.e. an informed guess!) for a sequence of letters of the plain-text from a message that corresponded to a sequence of letters from the cipher-text.

These cribs relied upon the likely occurrence of stereotyped phrases that had occurred in previous messages that had been broken. Some signals could be identified as 'routine' messages from their call-signs, times of transmission, and length, and these were the ones most likely to contain stereotyped text. Clearly there was a high degree of uncertainty about the accuracy of any straight crib, and unfortunately the only way of testing them was to try them out on the Bombes.

Often very fine judgments had to be made about which of several alternative possible cribs should be chosen for subsequent testing, bearing in mind the need to avoid as far as was possible the waste of valuable Bombe time.

'Depth' cribs:- These were derived from two messages that had both been transmitted on the same day and enciphered using *'message settings'* that happened to be nearly the same. Although cribs of this type were less forthcoming and took longer to prepare, they were much more likely to be accurate than a straight crib. However in order to be able to construct cribs of this type it was essential that the bi-gram tables currently in use were available.

An illustrative example of a 'Depth' crib is given in appendix (v).

Cribs derived from re-encodements:- These were based upon the discovery that some of the Enigma enciphered messages that had been intercepted had also been re- transmitted after having being enciphered by means of another (and simpler) hand-cipher that BP could break. Thus the plain-text from one of these broken signals could then be matched up with the characters of the corresponding (unbroken) Enigma cipher to produce a crib. Probably the most important examples were the weather reports that were regularly transmitted the by U-boats operating in the North Atlantic. These were subsequently re-broadcast (in another cipher by a shore based station) for general use by the German Navy.

The breaking of this second cipher (known as the *'dockyard cipher'*) enabled cribs to be constructed that could then be used to find Enigma keys.

Breaking the U-boat Ciphers

During the first eighteen months or so of the war the U-boats used the same Enigma system as the surface ships of the German Navy (i.e. 'Dolphin'), and consequently during this period there were no other additional problems to contend with in breaking their signals.

However from April 1941 the Enigma keys used by the Atlantic U-boats began to differ slightly from 'Dolphin', and information from various sources indicated that it was likely that a more advanced type of Enigma machine, known as 'M4', would soon be brought into operational use.

This machine had a fourth 'rotor' that could be pre-set to any one of twenty-six fixed positions. The term 'rotor' is perhaps somewhat misleading as in fact this device never moved from the position to which it was initially set. In effect this meant that the M4 Enigma machine operated with three true rotors and any one of twenty-six different reflectors that were made available by changing the pre-set position of the '4th rotor'. With twenty-six possible reflectors to test, the time required to check menus on the Bombes was increased by the same factor, and consequently there was an urgent need for the development of a high speed '4-rotor' version of the Bombe to cope with this new situation.

The change over to the M4 Enigma machine occurred on 1st February 1942, and at the same time a new Enigma key (known as *'Shark'*) was introduced for the exclusive use of the Atlantic U-boats, as a consequence, for many months following these changes BP were unable to break the U-boat signals

The characteristics of the M4 machine had previously been discovered as a result of a security blunder made by an Enigma operator some weeks before, but there were other difficulties that prevented this valuable information from being put to immediate use.

As the Atlantic U-boats were now using a different Enigma key from the rest of the German Navy, the re-enciphered weather reports became the only remaining source of cribs. In the previous months it had been possible to find cribs because BP had in their possession a captured copy of the *'Short signal weather code'* book that the Germans used to reduce the length of the weather reports that they transmitted (the indicators for these signals had been reduced to a single letter.)

Unfortunately on the 1st of January 1942 the Germans had introduced a new version of this code book and so, when they were most needed, the re-transmitted weather signals could no longer be used as a source of cribs.

A further serious problem created by the introduction of the M4 machine, was that even if accurate cribs had been available, there were no 4-rotor bombes to test them on. It was possible to improvise such a machine using a standard 3-wheel bombe, but the operating speed could not be increased and consequently the time taken to complete a test was much too long, unless a number of the machines were made available so that the huge task could be divided up between them.

For some months little progress was made against '*Shark*', but in October 1942 a copy of the new edition of the '*Short signal weather code*' book, together with lists of message indicator tables, were captured from U-559.

This crucial event took place at the cost of the lives of Lieutenant Anthony Fasson and Able Seaman Colin Grazier both members of the crew of the destroyer H.M.S. 'Petard'.

Other documents captured at the same time included a copy of the '*Short signal code*' book. This book was used when signals were transmitted by U-boats giving details of the position, course and speed of convoys that had been sighted.

After the captured copy of the new weather code book arrived at BP it was again possible to derive cribs from re-encoded weather reports in the way previously described, but the fact remained that the U-boat short signals were now being enciphered on M4 Enigma machines, although the captured lists of message indicators only gave three of the four wheel positions that would be expected for the M4 '*message settings*'.

A large number of trial tests based upon new cribs were then carried out using 3-rotor bombes as slow improvisations of 4-rotor machines, and after nearly three weeks of intensive effort involving many unsuccessful trials, a correct Enigma key was recovered. From this key it was found that the weather reports were always enciphered with the fourth rotor in the M4 machines pre-set to one particular position so that the machines functioned as M3 (3-rotor) versions of Enigma. This explained why the captured list of indicators only specified the setting of three of the rotors

This most important discovery meant that all future cribs derived from the weather reports could be tested using the standard 3-wheel bombes currently available at BP, and so there was no immediate need for 4-rotor bombes to carry out this work.

It was also discovered that the Enigma keys used to encipher the operational orders transmitted to the U-boats from their Headquarters on shore were almost the same as the keys being used for the short signal weather reports. The only difference was that the fourth rotor was being set to one of the other twenty-five possible positions available. This meant that the recovery of these keys did not present a major problem, for once the corresponding short signal weather key had been found, then subsequent tests to find the position of the 4th rotor only involved checking the other twenty-five of its possible positions. This could be carried out very rapidly, and the complete 4-rotor 'Shark' key determined

In retrospect the evidence provided by the captured lists of short signal indicators (giving only three of the four rotor positions required for the 'message settings') might seem have be sufficient for BP to have inferred that it was likely that the short signals were being enciphered, as previously described, with the M4 machines pre set to the M3 mode. If BP had tested this conjecture first then there would have been no need to carry out the lengthy sequence of unsuccessful trials mentioned above.

The following is a quotation from a letter written to the author by a senior person who was involved in this work:- '... we ran that extravagantly without assuming that the M3 reflector was still in use. I think that we should have tried it on that assumption first before putting the bombe people to the chore of wiring up the 25 other possible reflectors.'

On the 10th March 1943 the Short signal weather code book was changed again and so once more the re-encoded weather reports could no longer be used.

Remarkably BP was able to recover from this new setback by constructing new cribs by means of the 'Short signal code book' that had also been captured.

These signals were not rebroadcast and the cribs had to be constructed from the information supplied by the Royal Navy, on the known positions of convoys, their courses and their speeds etc. These signals were also enciphered with the Enigma machines in the M3 mode and consequently BP could still make effective use of the 3-rotor bombes.

Some additional information about short signals is given an appendix (vi)

The role of the four-rotor Bombes:-

At the beginning of 1943 there were no 4-rotor bombes in operation at BP and consequently the only possible way in which 'Shark' messages could be broken depended upon cribs derived from the two captured short signal code books.

However this work was never easy and in April and May 1943 the difficulties increased further as larger numbers of the cribs derived from these 'short signals' contained errors and consequently failed to produce accurate cribs, and considerably increased the demands on the limited Bombe resources.

Providentially at about this time another source of cribs became available. The number of signals transmitted to the U-boats operating in the Arctic began to increase significantly and as these messages were enciphered using '**Dolphin**', (the Enigma system used before the introduction of '*Shark*') they could be broken with the three-rotor bombes. Some of these signals were also transmitted to the Atlantic U-boats after being enciphered on the '*Shark*' key. These re-encoded signals were longer than those based upon the short signal code book, so by matching the plain-text derived from the broken 'Dolphin' signals with the cipher-text of the corresponding '*Shark*' enciphered message, a longer and more reliable crib could be obtained. However in order to make speedy use of these cribs, four-rotor bombes were needed.

In late June the first successful result were obtained using a British high speed 4-rotor bombe, but with the limited technical and material resources then available, the production of these machines failed to meet the operational needs.

In July 1943 the 4-rotor bombes developed in the United States had their first success, and by the autumn of that year two additional machines were coming into operational use every month.

As the number of American bombes steadily increased the importance of their role in breaking '*Shark*' became progressively greater, and in the middle of 1944 the responsibility for recovering these keys passed to the United States.

Appendix (i)   **THE GERMAN NAVAL INDICATOR SYSTEM**

The operator selected a three letter indicator from a printed list and enciphered it by means of a given set of bi-gram tables. This procedure provided two groups of four letters which were included twice in the transmitted signal, appearing once before the beginning of the Enigma enciphered message and again after it. The details of the procedure are as follows:-

From a document known as the '*K-book*', the operator identified the lists of three letter indicators that had been prescribed for the day, and from one of them he chose at random an indicator, for example say:- 'Y K S', (this was known as the '*procedure indicator group*'). He then placed an additional randomly selected letter, say 'H', at the end of this three letter group. He next chose another three letter indicator from the lists, say 'G A R' (this was known as the '*cipher indicator group*'), and placed an additional random letter, say 'Z', at the front. The resulting pair of four-letter groups were then placed one above the other in the way shown in this example :- Z G A R
                                                                              Y K S H

Then from the bi-gram tables provided the operator selected the page designated for the day, and replaced the four vertical pairs of letters with another set of four vertical pairs, to give say:- D J A X
                                                                              V R F Q

These two letter groups were then re-arranged to give the new groups DVJR and AFXQ and these were included twice in the transmitted signal in the way previously described. (Note that these two groups of letters were NOT enciphered by the Enigma machine).

The operator obtained the '*message settings*' that were to be subsequently used on the Enigma machine by turning the rotors on his Enigma machine to the '*Grundstellung*' positions prescribed for the day and then entering the three letters of the '*procedure indicator group*' (Y K S) on the keyboard, the corresponding three lamps that lit revealed the three letters of the '*message settings*'.

The receiving operator re-arranged the four letter groups DVJR and AFXQ to recover:- D J A X   and then from the bi-gram tables:- Z G A R
              V R F Q   Y K S H

These were the two groups of four letters originally formulated by the sending operator and contained the '*procedure indicator*' (Y K S) for the message.

The '*message settings*' were then recovered from the '*procedure indicator*' in the way that has already been explained.

The BI-GRAM TABLES

These were issued to the Naval Enigma operators in the form of a book containing a number of different bi-gram tables, and they were given instructions that specified which of the tables from the book was to be used on a given day. Each table contained 26 x26 cells, arranged in 26 rows and 26 columns labeled

A – Z and every cell in the table contained a pair of letters. Part of a bi-gram table is shown below:-

	A	B	C	D	E	F	G	H	I	J	K	L	M	etc
A	RN	KW	FM	YE	NR	UC	KE	XU	PC	JP	BD	QI	HT	
B	IK	RT	EY	AK	OW	WQ	QA	ZZ	OG	HQ	GC	PR	CD	
C	KJ	PO	JV	BM	MZ	EK	KT	AZ	ND	TQ	GX	RE	WA	
D	PK	EZ	AW	JM	WB	XY	ZA	BS	MT	OE	FP	RI	VV	
E	TC	JX	OM	MJ	NY	AS	PU	WO	KA	GZ	CF	FK	LK	
F	I J	ZB	CR	TT	KL	JC	UB	YQ	NQ	WC	EL	TR	AC	
G	GA	SD	BK	MF	KI	ZH	BY	HH	TW	VU	TH	XH	YF	
etc														

The tables were used in the following way:- Suppose that the bi-gram replacement for the letter pair DF is required; this is given by the letter pair shown in the cell in row D and in column F of the table (i.e. XY).

The table illustrates the symmetrical nature of the bi-gram system, for example it shows that that the letter pair FK is to be replaced by EL and likewise that the letter pair EL is to be replaced by FK.

It is possible that the bi-gram replacement given in a table is in fact the same pair of letters and in the above table the letter pair GA is one such example.

At fairly infrequent intervals the German Navy would change the bi-gram tables. This created further difficulties for the code-breakers in Hut 8, as the new tables then had to be recovered by means of a lengthy process involving the comparison of the intercepted message indicators with the corresponding *message settings* found from broken keys. Alternatively there was always the hope (sometimes fulfilled) of recovering the tables by capture.

THE 'EINS' CATALOGUES

After setting up an Enigma machine with the key for a given day, the 'EINS' catalogue for that day could be constructed by first enciphering the four letters E I N S at each of the 17,576 possible rotor starting positions. All of the results obtained were then arranged in an alphabetical order to form the catalogue.

The illustrative example given below is a very small part of a contrived catalogue for a particular key showing only the first 168 results obtained. The Enigma key used was:- Reflector B: Rotor order: I , II, III : Ring-settings: BPR. Steckers: All letters were self-steckered (i.e. A/A, B/B C/C …etc) (Self-steckers were chosen to make it quicker for those interested to try out the catalogue with a computer emulation of an Enigma machine.)

AAAU	GCD	AFQI	HFG	ANJD	HRW	ASIW	IHK	AYZC	JGL	BFJB	GZU
AACK	HYD	AGEG	GVP	ANPR	FTW	ASJB	IBS	AZHM	FBX	BFQW	GSH
AAJR	GCX	AGFM	HZQ	ANRN	ILT	ASLG	HTD	AZPJ	HRD	BFQX	HRH
AAKL	HLW	AGKU	GVD	ANYF	ITA	ATCD	IBF	AZQV	HHG	BFTP	GNQ
AARI	IJF	AGOV	FSK	AOAM	IOJ	ATFA	IST	AZRN	IQK	BFVX	GXE
AAVJ	IUB	AGVG	GSD	AOGE	ISS	ATFT	HKA	AZTH	HBZ	BFWZ	HNU
ABAV	HXI	AGZL	HQN	AOOZ	GRL	ATHW	IYM	AZXO	HBM	BFXC	ICX
ABEQ	IJI	AHON	HPH	AOTK	FAZ	ATQC	FRB	BACX	HPT	BGFP	GAB
ABFM	IDQ	AHZX	GUE	AOWO	IXC	ATXF	IKE	BACY	GYV	BGGA	GPG
ABFR	GSJ	AJEZ	IPR	AOYD	HUK	AUJU	HGI	BASI	GQU	BGKC	GJY
ABQK	HKK	AJHC	IBR	APAA	IYW	AUOO	IIO	BAZP	GQE	BGMI	IDJ
ABZC	GFJ	AJPT	FUR	APBZ	GCC	AVAH	HSV	BBCZ	IMF	BGYQ	HXF
ACHG	HDP	AJST	HJK	APKH	ICO	AVED	GYZ	BBEP	IAQ	BHKT	IUZ
ACJK	FDV	AJZO	HCG	APSG	IOG	AVFX	HDT	BBJP	GMQ	BHOG	HIH
ACMY	HPO	AJGM	IXT	APTP	HKR	AVUZ	JHX	BBXU	HDV	BHRE	HHL
ACSL	IZT	AJWG	JFP	APUE	FAM	AWAQ	IYJ	BCHQ	GOJ	BHUN	HPP
ACUC	GTK	AKXO	IQE	AQGR	IOW	AWGA	HWR	BCQA	IWX	BHXG	HBR
ADKH	GAV	ALGG	HBP	AQIU	JGA	AWVD	IGG	BCUA	GFZ	BHXG	FAR
ADKI	HII	ALKY	IFM	AQLV	FTZ	AWXQ	GXA	BDBJ	IIN	BJFJ	FPN
ADMG	FCZ	ALMW	FUJ	ARAM	GOQ	AXEV	FSL	BEBY	IWT	BKPI	HVX
ADMP	GGT	ALOH	FPK	ARBG	HGP	AXGG	GLP	BEDM	GJV	BKSL	HPI
ADQG	HKD	ALVP	GIA	ARCB	HFR	AXHA	FDD	BEKR	FUY	BKVA	GUG
ADRO	FVW	ALXN	HMH	ARHG	FVP	AXOL	GFN	BESC	ICH	BLIR	IFU
ADTO	FCD	AMAU	GNR	ARKR	FZG	AXQZ	GWL	BEVK	IYA	BLKI	GJZ
AEBD	ILI	AMII	HZJ	ARLU	FAI	AXVL	IUN	BEXB	HFY	BLRO	FCR
AEBY	GZR	AMZM	HKO	ARTV	GDX	AXXR	FWK	BEXH	HGT	BLSE	GYC
AEPI	FDZ	ANDX	JFC	ASCX	HHT	AYUA	HGW	BEXK	IZJ	BMGN	HUP
AFEC	FTG	ANIV	GDV	ASFU	FPU	AYUP	FSR	BEYW	FAU	BMJK	HRV

Part of an EINS Catalogue showing the cipher groups AAAU to BMJK

To appreciate how the catalogues were used, consider the following example based upon the restricted example given above. Suppose that a message transmitted on the known key given above started with the cipher text:- WBYK TPRA WGAZ WYPR ... (Navy signals were transmitted in groups of four letters).

The task of finding the message settings required that successive searches had to be made through the catalogue checking in turn the following letter groups WBYK , BYKT, YKTP, KTPR, TPRA, PRAW, RAWG, AWGA, WGAZ, etc (i.e. stepping on by one letter each time) to see if one of the resulting groups of four letters occurred in the catalogue.

It will be observed that the letter group AWGA does occur in the catalogue, showing that with the Enigma rotors set to HWR then the letter group AWAG is enciphered as E I N S. By moving the rotors back by seven positions to correspond to the first character of the cipher-text, the original *message settings* are thus found to be HWK.

For a period during the war a new EINS catalogue, had to be prepared each day. As every catalogue contained 17,576 entries (26×26×26), a special machine known as the '*baby*' was constructed to carry out this considerable task. This machine punched the results onto Hollerith cards that subsequently had to be sorted into order so that a systematic search could then be carried out for the enciphered letter groups. These tasks were carried out by the Hollerith Section at BP using automatic punched card sorting equipment.

It is however on record that the first trial catalogue was in fact made by hand with the aid of a British emulation of an Enigma machine; a huge task that must have taken some time to complete. After it had become possible to regularly recover Naval Enigma keys by means of the Bombes it was essential that a much faster method had to be used to construct the catalogues, and the '*baby*' formed the basis of this.

Appendix (iv)   **'BANBURISMUS'**

The German Navy used the M3 Enigma machine in conjunction with a set of eight rotors, of which five were identical to those used by the German Army and Air Force, the other three being specific to the Navy. With eight rotors the number of possible rotor orders was 336, for which menus would have required over 100 hours testing time on the Bombes. The resources available to BP were insufficient to meet this requirement and a way had to be found to reduce it.

Banburismus was a technique that made it possible to identify at least some of the Enigma rotors that had **not** been used during a particular two-day period, and this information significantly reduced the number of rotor orders that had to be tested on the Bombe. It was based upon the indicators of the intercepted messages, and in order to derive these from the repeated letter groups in these messages it was essential to have available the set of German Bi-gram tables currently in operational use.

The first objective was to recover parts of the so called *'Grundstellung alphabets'*. These were the three outcomes obtained by enciphering the 26 letters of the alphabet at each of the following three **fixed** positions of the rotors:-

'Grundstellung', *'Grundstellung + 1'*, *'Grundstellung + 2'*

The illustrative example of three such alphabets given below was obtained using an Enigma machine configured in the following way:-

Rotor order: 1, 5, 2 Reflector: 'B': Ringstellung: WQT : Grundstellung: PDS

Stecker pairs: A/G, B/U, C/H, D/L, E/I, F/R, K/P, M/S, Q/W, V/Z.

(*'Grundstellung'* = PDS: *'Grundstellung + 1'* = PDT: *'Grundstellung + 2'* = PDU)

The three Alphabets

Rotor Settings	A	B	C	D	E	F	G	H	I	J	K	L	M	N	O	P	Q	R	S	T	U	V	W	X	Y	Z
'PDS'	M	E	I	S	**B**	K	R	Y	C	T	F	P	A	O	N	L	V	G	D	J	W	Q	U	Z	H	X
'PDT'	M	**K**	I	F	G	D	E	R	C	N	B	V	A	J	X	U	S	H	Q	Y	P	L	Z	O	T	W
'PDU'	Y	O	D	C	H	S	M	E	W	K	J	X	**G**	U	**B**	R	Z	P	F	V	N	T	I	L	A	Q

The following notes show how part of the 'Grundstellung + 2' alphabet (i.e. obtained at the fixed rotor positions PDU) shown above, can be recovered from a number of pairs of intercepted messages with indicators that only differ in their right hand letters. Once this has been accomplished then it becomes possible to make some extremely useful deductions that greatly reduced the number of possibilities for the rotor that could have been located in the right-hand position in the Enigma machines when these messages had been enciphered.

With the aid of the bi-gram tables the indicators of the intercepted messages could be found from the included repeated letter groups described in appendix (i).

The work began by selecting from all the intercepts those pairs of signals for which only the third letters of the indicators were different, EBM and EBW for example.

For such a pair of indicators only the third letters of the corresponding (but unknown) message settings would be different, and so the 'difference' between the message settings could be measured as the difference between the numerical positions that these letters occupied in the standard alphabetic order (A B C ..... Z); this value was known as the '*offset*'

For example consider the pair of indicators EBM and EBO. The Grundstellung alphabets given above show that the two corresponding message settings are:- BKG and BKB, so that the message with the indicator EBO has an offset of 5 (i.e. measuring from B to G) 'in front' of the message with the indicator EBM.

Note: It must be remembered that at the time both the configuration of the Enigma machine and the Grundstellung alphabets would have been unknown, and so the offsets between pairs of message settings could not have been found in this way.

In order to overcome this difficulty a statistical method was developed that made it possible to obtain estimates for the offsets without needing any prior knowledge of the configuration of the Enigma machine or of the Grundstellung positions. This method was based on the probable statistical characteristic of the plain-text of the messages.

It is an established fact that if two rows of random sequences of letters from the alphabet are aligned one above the other so as to produce vertical pairs of letters, then the expected proportion of the pairs in which both letters are the same will be 1/26.

If however the two random sequences of letters are replaced by sequences of letters from different passages of German (or English) plain-text, then the corresponding proportion of the pairs in which both letters are the same is significantly greater (approximately 1/15). This is a consequence of the fact that the frequency distribution of the letters in the plain-text is not random, as some letters are more likely to occur than others.

The characters of enciphered plain-text are in effect just sequences of random letters, and so in general if two enciphered messages are placed one above the other in the way described above, the expected proportion of pairs in which both letters are the same will be about 1/26.

However if parts of two messages both happen to have been enciphered on an Enigma machine that had configured in the same way and also with the same sequence of rotor positions, then when these two parts are aligned one above the other the expected proportion of vertical pairs in which both letters are the same will be about 1/15. The explanation for this is that vertical pairs of identical cipher-text letters will occur when the corresponding pairs of letters from the two sequences of plain-text are the same, and the expected proportion of these is 1/15.

Messages (or parts of them) that can be aligned in this way were said to have been 'aligned in depth'.

If one cipher message could be correctly aligned in depth with part of another, then it became possible to measure the offset between their starting positions.

For pairs of messages where the indicators differed only in the third place, the process of alignment was carried out by hand using specially printed material known as 'Banburies'. These were long strips of thick paper about 10 inches wide and several feet long on which all the letters of the alphabet (A – Z) had been printed repeatedly in columns across the width. The alphabet columns on a sheet were used consecutively one by one to match the sequence of letters from the cipher-text, a hole being punched in each column of the sheet over the corresponding letter from the cipher-text. Two completed sheets (one for each message) were then aligned by placing one on top of the other on a very long table and sliding the top one laterally in turn to each of the possible relative starting positions. At each of these positions, pairs of identical letters were detected visually by the coincidence of pairs of holes, and so could easily be counted. The relative position giving the highest score of identical letter pairs was taken as the 'best estimate' of the offset.

The following results were obtained using a particular pair of messages.

Two different passages of English plain text each consisting of approximately 250 characters, were enciphered on an Enigma machine, (set up with the configuration and Grundstellung given earlier) using the two message settings:- BKS and BKZ

(Note: the 1st message setting has an offset of 7 in front of the 2nd one).

By means of a computer emulation the two sequences of cipher characters were then aligned at a number of different offsets, and counts obtained of the occurrence of coincident pairs of letters. These results are shown in the following table:-

Offset	Coincident pairs	Offset	Coincident Pairs	Offset	Coincident Pairs
0	10	9	8	18	7
1	7	10	13	19	4
2	10	11	8	20	16
3	10	12	12	21	12
4	12	13	9	22	9
5	9	14	14	23	6
6	9	15	9	24	8
7	**21**	16	13	25	6
8	5	17	10		

This table shows a value of '7' to be the 'best estimate' for the offset, which in this case, happens to coincide with the true value given earlier. In practice there was a level of uncertainty about the accuracy of the estimates obtained by means of the Banbury sheets and a mathematical procedure was developed to calculate the numerical odds that a 'best estimate' was in fact correct. These odds were then used in the next stage of the work. (Some information about this is given later.)

The Banburismus procedure required that first a number of offsets between pairs of messages were estimated by means of the 'Banburies'. Each offset was then represented by the right-hand letters of the corresponding pair of message

This leads to the elimination of all the other rotors with the exception of rotor II, as this has its notch position outside the span of all the offsets. Hence rotor (II) must have occupied the right-hand position.

With this information and without taking any other possible restrictions into account, the number of possible rotor orders that remain to be tested on the Bombe is reduced from 336 to 42 (7 x 6), a spectacular reduction.

Finding the odds that a derived 'Grundstellung alphabet' is correct:-

The example given above explains how the Banbury sheets were used, but it fails to address a very difficult question about the resulting Grundstellung alphabets.

It has been emphasized that all the offsets used in the example were 'certain', but that during the War only 'best estimates' for the offsets obtained from the message indicators would have been available and there was the possibility that one or more of them could be wrong. Consequently it was important to be able to determine the likelihood (measured in terms of the mathematical odds) that these offsets, and the 'Grundstellung alphabets' subsequently derived from them, were correct so that the alphabets had sufficiently high level of 'credibility' to enable them to be used with confidence.

Alan Turing was responsible for the development of a highly sophisticated mathematical procedure that addressed this question. It was based upon the concept of the *weight of evidence* needed to support the belief that a Grundstellung alphabet derived from a number of estimated offsets was in fact 'certain'.

The basic idea was to choose an appropriate numerical value for the *weight of evidence* required, and then progressively to combine together the information provided by the offsets until the resulting *combined weight of evidence* reached the desired level of credibility. In order to achieve this it was necessary to have acquired about dozen or more offsets, with the majority having high measures of credibility.

`Sometimes during the work a particular offset would be found to provide information that was inconsistent with that provided by the majority of the others.

When this occurred this offset would be rejected, and a negative contribution made to the *'combined weight of evidence'* (i.e. reducing the measured level of credibility).

The final numerical value obtained was a measure of the mathematical odds that the alphabet was in fact correct, and odds of about '50 to 1 on' were considered to be adequate for it be regarded as 'certain'.

The mathematical procedures used to carry out this work were also applied to solve some problems of a similar nature that occurred later at BP in the breaking of the 'Fish' ciphers with Colossus. After the war this innovative technique became known as 'Sequential Analysis'.

Appendix (v)   **DEPTH CRIBS**

Note: The reader should be familiar with the material on 'Banburismus' given in Appendix (iv) before proceeding further.

Sometimes a Depth crib could be derived from two intercepted messages that had been enciphered with the same Enigma key, for which the letters in two message settings differed only at the right-hand position. For reasons explained elsewhere, in order to recover the message indicators from the letter groups included in the intercepted signals, the current set of the German bi-gram tables had to be available.

If only the right-hand letters of two message indicators were different then only the right-hand letters of the message settings would be different. Suppose that for such a pair of such messages, the first has been identified with reasonable certainty as a routine signal likely to contain a particular form of words. (Such messages could often be identified by their call signs, and the times of transmission.) Then if the two messages could be aligned with one another at the correct offset, so that if the two sequences of plain-text letters had common letters at some positions, so would the two sequences of cipher-text letters.

For example the following pair of cipher messages with:-

Indicator   Opening Cipher letters
  YAJ   XXUFHIPFWBGQQXQVKH……..
  YAU   TIBUBJBZOQXQVKLBTGOQC……….

The best estimate for the offset between this pair of messages is the one when the first message is 3 positions 'in front' of the second one.

This particular alignment of the two messages is shown below.

X X U F H I P F W **B** G Q **Q** **X** **Q** **V** **K** H

       T I B U B J **B** Z O **Q** **X** **Q** **V** **K** L B T G O Q C

The appearance of six pairs of common letters in the aligned messages is a very strong indication that the alignment is correct.

It then follows that the alignment of the two corresponding sequences of plain-text letters will also contain six pairs of common letters.

Suppose that the conjectured crib for the first (routine) message is:-

WETTERFUERDIENACHT   ('*Weather for the night ....*')

This sequence of letters can then be matched with the corresponding letters of cipher-text:-

W E T T E R F U E R D I E N A C H T
X X U F H I P F W B G Q Q X Q V K H
    T I B U B J B Z O Q X Q V K L B T G O Q C

The underlined pairs of cipher-text/plain-text letters can now be used to establish some of the plain text-letters from the second message:-

W E T T E R F U E R D I E N A C H T
X X U F H I P F W B G Q Q X Q V K H
    T I B U B J B Z O Q X Q V K L B T G O Q C
    F ? ? ? ? ? R ? ? E N A C H ? ? ? ? ? ? ?

Note that the letter F at the 1st position in the second message can also be identified. This is a consequence of good fortune as it happens that T has been enciphered as F at the 4th position in the first message.

The plain-text letters from the second message that have been now been recovered are very plausible, and consequently the chosen crib can be regarded as certainly correct. It is a matter of speculation whether the skill people working in Hut 8 would have deduced the second message from the incomplete fragment given above. This actually message begins:-

FUERMARINENACHRICHTEN...... (*For Naval Communications.....*)

Generally the work was not as straightforward as this example might suggest, and there were occasions when even after a great deal of effort a crib was not found.

Depth cribbing and Banburismus had much in common. After September 1943, as circumstances changed with more bombes becoming available, both procedures ceased to be used.

Appendix (vi)   **SHORT SIGNALS**

In order to reduce the chances of detection by British high frequency direction finding, the U-boats operating in the Atlantic only transmitted short signals. The structure of these signals depended upon two designated codebooks:-

(I) '*Wetterkertzschlussel*' (Weather short signal code book)

(II) '*Kurtzsignalheft*' (Short signal code book) used to send operational information.

An example of a 'Weather short signal':-

W W   F S Z E Q R A E H P G U

A brief explanation:-

W W:- Call sign to indicate a 'Weather short signal'.

F:-   Indicator (reference letter for the *message settings* given in a printed list)

The remaining letters form the weather report after it had been encoded by means of the 'Weather short signal' code book that enabled each item of meteorological data to be expressed as a single letter.

S and Z:- Latitude and longitude (degrees).

E:- Change in barometric pressure over a statutory period of time.

Q and R:- Current barometric pressure and air temperature.

A:- Current wind direction and strength. E:- Current weather and cloud.

H:- Visibility. P:- Direction and type of ocean swell.

GU:-   The U-boat signature (used to establish its identity).

An example of an operational 'Short signal':-

β β OOD QLTI SCYK AZEE TNFX OJ

A brief explanation:-

β β :- Call sign used to indicate an operational 'Short signal'.

Note: In the German Naval morse code used at the time b = ¾ · · · ¾

(This became known to the British as 'B bar')

OOD :- The message indicator (used with a 'look up' table to find the message settings.)

Cipher group: QLTI, Decode: CKSA Meaning: *Enemy convoy sighted*
Cipher group: SCYK, Decode: KBXO Meaning: BE 41 (1st map reference)
Cipher group: AZEE, Decode: MBGV Meaning: 31 (2nd map reference)
(The U-boats had Marine charts for use with these references)

Cipher group: TNFX, Decode: QQYY Meaning: *Course towards South*
Cipher group: OJ, Decode: YN Meaning: U-276 (U-boat signature)

(The meanings of these decoded letter groups were obtained from the captured operational *Short signal* code book.)

For both types of short signals the letters following on after those of the call signs and indicators would be enciphered on an Enigma machine (set to the appropriate key) before the signal was transmitted. Hence any crib derived from a 'WW' signal would at most consist of only eleven letter pairs and this was about the absolute minimum number necessary to achieve success in the subsequent work carried out on the bombes.

Deriving cribs from the short signals:-

Some of the letter groups that occurred in the operational short signals could be deduced by using the captured 'short signal' code book in conjunction with the current information about the known position, course and speed of the convoys at sea as provided by the Royal Navy. However it was often not possible to succeed for all of the letter groups and consequently the number of letters in a crib obtained from one signal were often insufficient for use with the Bombes.

It was sometimes possible to combine the letter groups from more than one signal. This could be done because the indicator tables used for both types of signals had been captured. With the information from these tables the message settings that had been used for the intercepted signals could be found. Hence if two or more signals with suitable message settings had been intercepted, these could be aligned 'in depth' and a stronger crib derived from them. This work was never easy, and quite frequently such a crib would contain inaccuracies, resulting in unsuccessful Bombe trials. However it is on record that on the occasion of the first successful break back into '*Shark*' three or four 'WW' signals had been aligned in this way.
